Reset

Andrew Aldred

chipmunkapublishing
the mental health publisher

Andrew Aldred

Published by
Chipmunkapublishing
United Kingdom

http://www.chipmunkapublishing.com

ISBN   978-1-78382-6971

Dedicated To Jane

Andrew Aldred

Holy Site

There is a holy site in Jerusalem.
Where the fighting never stops
You should know we are all God's chosen people.
We are all equal in most ways.
And one race is no better than another.
Now the holy war has come back.
And Israels prime minister drones on
About the war of all wars
Half the Arab world is out on the streets.
Howling for the blood of Americans and Israelis
Will we ever learn to live together?
Can there ever be a lasting peace?
You cannot blame the next generation of Palestinians.
For wanting to support Hamas and the terrorists
Their homes were obliterated, and they have nothing.
Israel has already killed three times as many.
As Hamas killed of their people
Yet they still want to occupy Gaza?
And they think they will kill every member of Hamas.
Something terrible has come to this region.
And it will only ever end in tears for everybody.
What the hell do all these people pray for?
Does peace matter to anyone in the middle east?

Andrew Aldred

The Failure of Multiculturalism?

Suella Braverman comes out with some sweeping statements.
She thinks multiculturalism has failed in this country.
Because of the influx of people coming over in boats
But as I see it this is absolutely not the case
The UK is in fact a multicultural and racially integrated success.
Because everybody has their say, and we are all accepted.
Every European country wants to limit the number of refugees.
But there needs to be some co-operation between all countries.
To take in a proportionate number, and that includes us.
Whether we are part of the European Union or otherwise
We cannot opt out of our responsibilities to the world.
Multiculturalism is a good idea and can be a great success.
We can all live together in one country and get along.

Getting on with Living

I am far too busy getting on with living.
To be bothered with thinking about dying
Believe in extinction rebellion and just stop oil.
And to some extent I can see their point
But nature also has a huge play in things.
The climate does alter and always has.
The human race does not drive everything on the planet.
Nature will correct herself over time.
We are running out of fossil fuels anyway.
Re-usable energy will power everything in the future.
Responsible conservation is happening because people care.
About green issues, conservation and the environment
Greta Thunberg can spend her life in and out of jail.
But I will be getting on the best I can.
The weather will change, and evolution will take place.
And I will keep up with change if I am able to

Endless War

We now have two wars that will not go away.
Ukraine and Russia are still going at it.
And so are Israel and Hamas in the East
I do not see any clear victory for anyone.
Just long and drawn-out conflict for years
Ukraine might drive Russia out of their country.
And Israel might drive Hamas out of Gaza.
But will there ever be a lasting peace?
These wars have been going on for years before now.
The children will grow up and fight them all over again.
Everyone is too concerned with their own point of view.
To consider burying the hatchet and living together
It seems people just want to fight it out in an endless war.
Did it ever have to be like this in the first place?

Hostile Environment

The rains came down in Eastern Scotland last night.
Angus and Brechin were drenched and submerged in water.
Extreme weather events are happening everywhere now.
Driving a car is enough of a risk without the storms.
And if we must stay indoors that is what we will do
The seasons are out of synchronisation this year.
Summer is creeping into Autumn and the temperatures have risen.
We have seen drought and flooding at different times of the year.
I am so glad we do not live on the coast or near a river.
But England's green and pleasant land can be hostile at times.

Wrangling

The estate agent got an offer for her mother's house.
But then they decided to do a homebuyer's survey
And they came up with all sorts of reasons to lower the price.
The fact is that they have not quite got the money to buy it.
The estate agent valued it and so did two others.
And we cannot accept twenty thousand pounds below the price.
They have withdrawn their offer, and we are no further forward.
We cannot give things away for the good of everybody else.
Money is tight and people will be wrangling over house prices.

Sovereign Nations

As sovereign nations we cannot tell each other what to do.
If we went to war over anything we would not want that
We are not able to dictate anything to Israel or Hamas
And that is the point that thousands of people protesting.
Do not understand, as well as the labour leader is partly Jewish.
The current leaders of Israel and Hamas want this fight.
And we all wish they would stop but they are going to fight.
Everybody needs to stand back and let them get on with it.
We are supporting Israel in some ways while we give Palestine aid.
We are an island many miles away and in no position to take charge.
The Americans are only defending their own interests in the middle east.
And have respectfully told Israel to consider what they are doing.
Israel will not make itself popular anywhere with what it has done.
The rest of the world will judge them a long time after this war.

Andrew Aldred

Floundering

There is a new national epidemic called suicide.
All that is keeping a lot of people alive is a handful of tablets.
I am one of those and have been for forty years.
My sister would not accept help and sadly died.
I have been watching Roman Kemp's campaign on TV.
And it seems mental health is very important for the young
But myself and some people I know are too far gone.
My mental health prevents me from doing paid work.
The world of employment seems impossible to break into
If there are too many people like me the country will grind to a
halt
I try to look after myself and Jane and that is more than enough.
They do not want the likes of me to work for them these days.
My advice to you is do what you can while you can.
Try to make the most of every opportunity before it is taken away.
One day you will end up treading water that is very deep.
And continually threatens to engulf and drown you.

The New Holy War?

Hezbollah has just said they are prepared to be involved.
Whilst giving all the glory for the idea to Hamas
Iran is going to be in the background at the very least.
Supplying Hezbollah with weapons and wanting Israels destruction
Wanting America to get involved so scores can be settled.
It looks like all hell will break loose in this new holy war.
Just as Israels' prime minister said only far worse.
There seem to be no end of people wanting to die for Allah.
What is the Jihad about anyway? Can we not just forget it?
Can we not live in peace? Does there have to be a war?
And now they are marching on London every Saturday expectantly.
But Hamas did not rape and mutilate women and children.
To have a ceasefire a few weeks later for humanitarian reasons.
There are a lot of Jews in this country as well as Palestinians.
The labour party could lose a potential prime minister over this.
Are we really supposed to bow down to the Muslim community?
This is a complex and divisive issue for everybody involved.
I thought we had stopped locking up Muslim clerics and deporting them.
But we may have to deal with this and terrorism all over again.
The war in the middle east is not going away.

Andrew Aldred

Worry About Us

Scotland's prime minister has been all over the news.
Talking about his mother and father-in-law in Palestine
Many labour politicians are talking about resigning.
Because of the stance their leader is taking over the war
But they all live here and need to get on with their jobs.
The labour party needs to show solidarity if it wants power.
Humza Yousef needs to think about running Scotland.
We could all do without thousands protesting on a Saturday.
Whether it is peaceful and within the law or otherwise
We certainly do not want a new wave of terrorists over here.
We have a cost-of-living crisis and freak weather events.
This winter will be bleak enough in Britain without anything else.
I am so sick of people trying to tread the moral high ground.
This is where we live so let's make things better here.

Reset

I wish we could go back to a time before the freak weather.
I wish we could go back to a time when there was no war.
When people were better off and there was hope for the young
I wish we could have no racism and no people with guns.
I wish I had friends in this desolate town.
I wish my bank balance would go up instead of down.
If we could somehow reset everything and make it alright
A better world might be within sight.

Way Too Far

People always think they can do just what they want.
And that nobody will notice they are all psychopaths
Hamas attacked Israel and raped, mutilated and murdered people.
And now the Israelis have blown up most of Gaza.
The Americans are trying to calm down the madness and so are
we.
With talk of safe areas, aid and humanitarian corridors
But America has already sent a nuclear submarine over.
Hezbollah, Libya and Iran are hiding in the background.
I believe this situation has always been out of control.
And because of the division and hatred will only get worse
A series of poorly thought-out military strikes and bad decisions
Has produced a situation where everybody has gone way too far.

Ten Miles

There has been a lot of fighting around Kherson recently.
Between the Ukrainians and Russians with heavy losses
Ukraine is determined but has only progressed ten miles.
The situation is a stalemate, and both sides are tired.
Western governments have supplied Ukraine with arms until now.
But there is war in the middle east and priorities have changed.
Most Ukrainians believe they will drive Russia out of the country.
But they are not progressing with achieving that now.
Could Russia and Ukraine ever broker a ceasefire now?
Does the situation have to be fought down to the last man?
And the last bullet, will they ever call it a day?
Ten miles in six months speaks for itself. No real progress

Andrew Aldred

Goodbye Psychiatrist

I went to see the psychiatrist the other day.
For the first time in nearly ten years
He listened while I answered his questions.
He said he wanted me to have an ECG.
And if the results were satisfactory, I would be discharged.
I went to the GP and let the nurse take my readings.
She relayed the results to my GP and my psychiatrist.
And then she said I could go so I went
Goodbye psychiatrist. I guess you have had enough of me.

Hideous Woman

It is not how she looks it is what she says.
That continually annoys people and grabs headlines.
Let's hope you can put your jackboots in your bag.
And let somebody else have a go at doing your job.
First it is sending refugees to a dumping ground in Rwanda.
Then it is saying that multiculturalism has failed in this country
After that she claims that homelessness is a lifestyle choice
And she tops it all off with incendiary remarks about Palestinians.
Wanting to stir up racial hatred and create problems for the police.
She is a person who needs to spend time on the streets.
Being evicted and having no money or means to support herself.
She needs to be repatriated somewhere else for her own good.
Does she think she is right or is she laughing at everyone?
I believe this woman is a danger to herself and everybody else.
And politics is the wrong job for her and those like her.

No Long-Term Solutions

There is no solution in sight to the problems in Gaza.
There is no agreement to what will happen after the war.
There is no moral high ground. Both sides are in the wrong
Gaza will have to be rebuilt. Who will pay for it?
What will happen to Palestinians? Where will they go?
Hamas is an ideology. How will the Israelis get rid of it?
Will Israel and Gaza ever be able to co-exist after this?
Will the hostages ever be released given the way Israel is
behaving?
I see no solutions. Just a lot of problems that will not go away.

Get Them Paid

They are a high-octane breed of men.
Builders, labourers and men who work on rooftops.
They earn a lot of money, and they spend it as well.
We have had a team of men working on her rooftop.
They have worked tirelessly for three days now.
It is the end of another hard day and they have finished.
They want to be paid now so they can sign the job off.
So, I drive home and get on my computer as quick as I can.
It wants to update and then it crashes taking extra time.
I keep on with it and then must change the settings.
And I do the transaction just as the phone starts ringing.
I tell her I have had problems, and the payment is through.
After a while I phone her, and they have gone away happy.
We can breathe a sigh of relief and get on with our lives.

Staking His Reputation

Rishi Sunak is staking his reputation on this policy.
And I believe that it will either make him or break him.
He wants to make it possible to deport people to Rwanda.
If they have not come to Britain by legal means
His former home secretary has criticised him for not doing this.
And she wants him to alter the legal framework of this country.
It might mean ignoring the European Court of Justice
And going our own way with a lot of legal jurisdictions
I know a lot of people support this, but I do not.
The Geneva Convention laid down a lot of important rules.
And we should respect them like other countries do.
We all fought in the second world war, and this was the result.
We cannot rip up the rulebook because it does not suit our
purpose.
Boat crossings across the channel are down by a third this year.
Surely, we must take responsibility for some of these people.
Sunak has delivered on his economic policy, but can he do this?
I hope he sees a clear path through this problem and solves it.
And shuts up Braverman and Starmer in a palatable way.

Chasing Smoke

Israel has gone into Gaza with its tanks.
But the enemy is melting into the population.
They leave their guns and weapons to be found.
The Israelis might think they have won but they have not.
The terrorists will do the same as the Taliban.
And they will take over again once Israel has gone.
And the entire Palestinian population will be terrorists.
And if you are Jewish, you had better watch out.
They can blow the entire country up, but they are chasing smoke.

Andrew Aldred

Hot Air

There has been more speculation about this fight.
Then there would be about the second coming of Christ
The date was set and then the fight was postponed.
Tyson Fury seems to think that he is bigger than boxing.
While Usyk remains calm and focused on the future event
Fury has disrespected promoters and sports pundits alike.
Every world champion for the last thirty years has an opinion.
That they post on the internet as well as their glory days
Boxing is more of a circus than it has ever been.
There is far too much money and all they do is talk.
The fight could go either way, but it is all up to Tyson Fury
Will he put in the work or just turn up for the fight?
We really do not know and that is what is intriguing.
Until the fight gets underway all we will get is hot air

Ceasefire

There has been a ceasefire in Gaza for a week now.
Hostages on both sides have been freed.
Aid is coming into Gaza left, right and centre.
America and the rest of the world wants it to continue.
But Israel is intent on eradicating Hamas from Gaza
There are less and less hostages to be freed.
And Israel's prime minister wants to finish the job.
Will Israel ever see that it has done enough?
A country that has been razed to the ground.
And fifteen thousand dead should be a deterrent.
We pray for the ceasefire to continue but reality is brutal.

Monsters

A boy and a girl murdered a transgender person.
They planned it detail and named her as a target.
They left a disturbing trail of evidence behind them.
From the murder weapon to a previous attempt at killing her
These people were all only sixteen years old.
Whatever happened to peace, love and understanding?
It was nowhere to be seen when she was stabbed.
The boy and girl responsible need locking up forever.
There was no reason or excuse for this behaviour.
Monsters is too good a word to describe those who did this.

Christmas on the Cheap

We gave up buying branded clothes a long time ago.
We have not eaten out for a few years.
Let alone go on holiday or out for the night.
Supermarket brands are all we ever buy.
We are lucky to have enough money to fix the roof.
Or pay for a newer second-hand car occasionally.
We bought our Christmas presents in November this year.
While the prices were cheaper, and they had not sold out.
Heating and eating are costing more than ever before.
I am sorry to say I cannot see things getting any better
The government says they will, but I see no sign.
Money is harder and harder to save and goes quickly.
TV and social media give you a false view of life.
It will be Christmas on the cheap after another hard year.

OFSTED Inspection

The head teacher at the school killed herself.
And we know OFSTED inspections are subjective things.
You can get a set of sticklers coming to your school.
Or you can get people who condone everything you do.
Whether it is good, bad or indifferent.
There seems to me there was more to this suicide.
Anyone can lose a job and a reputation and recover.
But there are other factors that push people over the edge.
Suicide is an awful thing, and the truth dies with the dead.
And it is all too convenient to blame and inspection by OFSTED.

The End of a Generation

The elders in our family are coming to the end of their years.
I hope we can let them pass on without too many tears.
They all lived long and did what they wanted with no reservation.
But now it is our turn to do things our way without judgement.
Things will not be that different, but we will carry on without them.
They will be missed. They were loved although they were not always right.
They know us well by now and we could all be a lot worse
I hope the next life has some peace and rest for all of them.
And they do not suffer too much as they near the end.
It is the end of their generation. We will be the next to go.

Guilty

Israels prime minister is guilty of a lot.
Killing Palestinians to get what he has got.
There's more and more of these people dying.
There are more and more children who are crying.
Without mothers and fathers, and brothers and sisters
Bombed and displaced without food to eat.
Walking for miles to safety on sore feet
They have bombed the country leaving nothing.
I wish to God somebody would do something.
To make this situation better than it is
The world is turning a blind eye to people in crisis.
Israel has gone way too far for me.
I look at my television and tragedy are all I see.

Defining Policy

This is Rishi Sunak's defining policy.
Will he be able to send people to Rwanda or not?
I would have given up on this a long time ago.
Everything must be dragged through court and is so slow.
There are no houses for our own people to live in
They are requisitioning old barracks for the refugees.
As well as offshore barges and anything they can fit them in
You can stop the boats, but they are still coming in.
But we are full to capacity and there is no space.
After this I do not see how Rishi Sunak can remain in power

The Council is Bankrupt

Councils are bankrupt and it is all over the news.
Turning on lights instead of fixing roads
Everything needs to be stripped down to the essentials.
As people donating to food banks turn to using them
Poverty trickles down as the rich become the new poor.
No money for adult or youth services any more
They are not emptying the bins over in Warrington.
People have had enough so keep your head down.
The council is bankrupt and so are the rest of us.

Farce

It is the biggest farce I have seen on TV.
They are trying to make them accountable for the pandemic.
All the relatives of the dead are looking on.
But Boris Johnson cannot bring their loved ones back.
It was all he could do to survive COVID himself.
Everyone knows what we did wrong during the pandemic.
Putting this circus on TV is such a pointless exercise.
Would you want to run a government during a pandemic?
Most of us have enough problems with the life we have got.
People live and die every day and life goes on.
We can sift through the evidence of anything forever.
But sooner or later people need to lay things to rest.
I am sick of public enquiries, and I wish people would let things
be.

Look After Yourself

My brother really has his work cut out this year.
He has recently been diagnosed with haemochromatosis.
And this means he has to give blood once a week.
Until his iron levels are within normal range
He is also working hard collecting rubbish for the council.
And my elderly parents, although in a care home
Depend on my brother for a lot of their needs.
I would like to help but live many miles away.
The only advice I can give him is to look after himself.
And like him I will try to remain well over Christmas.
And not bother the Doctor or the hospital if at all possible
Jane will be the only family I have this Christmas.
All the best to everyone else and please keeps well.

Future Wars

Vladimir Putin has made his intentions clear today.
After he has taken Ukraine there will be peace
President Zelensky is telling everyone they are next.
Zelensky is failing in its bid to secure arms and money.
And Ukraine is on the second page after what is going on in Gaza.
And then there is the mess in Syria that needs cleaning up.
Will Russia ever stop aggressively going after new land?
What was the point in Ukraine fighting Russia in the first place?
If Putin wins, we are all going to look hopeless and stupid.
And aggressive states will think they can do what they want.
The implications of these wars are not good for the rest of us.
We have neither the money nor the will to stand up for what is
right.
Any number of states could be at war in the near future.

Soldier F

They are making him stand trial for murder after fifty years.
A parachute regiment soldier caught up in the bloody Sunday riots.
He has no clear recollection of what happened that day.
But may spend the rest of his life paying for his actions.
If mobs did not parade through streets causing trouble
Sticking two fingers up at authority this would not have happened.
But then again was the response to the civil unrest reckless?
Were people indiscriminately shot just because they were there?
This has cost the taxpayer two hundred million in legal fees.
And it is another historical event that just will not go away.
And it will turn out very unfortunate for anyone who was there?

Computer Generation

This generation do things differently. Everything is computer controlled.
If they want to write a poem, they put the details in a computer.
If they want to write a song, they get the software to do it.
Everything is sampled and the computer arranges it and puts it together.
There are no more guitar heroes. They are a thing of the past.
People do not play instruments. They sing through a synthesiser.
You need a level of knowledge to be able to do all of this.
You need to know how things are constructed and have a vision.
Of what you are trying to create and what it will look and sound like
People used to gather in social settings. Computers have taken over.
You are never alone in your house. There is always Alexa.
Everything is simulated. There is no need for reality anymore.
You can play call of duty instead of going to war.
But of course, there is no substitute for real skills.
And the people that have them will always have money.
You can have a million followers but how does that turn into cash?
You can have a computer but what would you do if it were to crash?

Andrew Aldred

Just You and Me

The kids have got their own lives and all they want is money.
My relatives are getting on with things two hundred miles away.
Your mother is in a care home getting on with dying slowly.
The friends we had have long since gone their own way.
Your sister is getting on with her own family this year.
So, its just you and me, the cat and the television
We visited your mother and had a WhatsApp conversation.
With your sister, her husband and your niece and nephew
We managed to cook our Christmas meal on boxing day.
Your daughter might get back to us and we will see our grandson.
In the New Year, all being well. I hope he has been good.
Just you and me this year darling, we are growing old.

Guitar Playing Nut

I have been dreaming for years.
Of buying another guitar
I sold all the ones I had.
And got a job to pay the bills.
But recently the day arrived.
And this time my girlfriend approves.
I played it all night when I got it.
For two days and my fingers blistered
I popped them with a needle.
I think it is the best thing I have bought.
And I guess that I'm a guitar playing nut.

Sober Christmas

I stopped drinking last January.
We made it through Christmas 2023
And for a change there were no disasters
No distractions and nothing to go wrong.
To tell the truth I do not miss it at all.
Although I could not have got through without it
Like cigarettes it makes me sick these days
After forty years I wonder why I bothered
And realise I had to so I could get here.
I hope next year is another sober Christmas.

Columbus

It's a Columbus in cherry sunburst.
It was the best guitar I could afford.
It's a copy of a well-known Gibson.
And it's been expertly handcrafted in Korea.
By people paid a lot less that Americans
Its coming to me in a box from Bristol
I spent ages looking on the internet.
This was the right price and I wanted it.
I used to have one back in the day.
It's a Columbus in cherry sunburst.
And it will be coming today or tomorrow.

Andrew Aldred

Tearing the World to Bits

You see the Jews and the Palestinians
Then see the NHS and the government.
You know what is going on with the neighbours.
And you realise they are all full of shit.
Everybody wants to think they are in charge.
And they will not let the people get on.
They always want to take it out on us.
When they are all so badly behaved
You learn to despair of them and ignore them.
They have so little in their sad lives
All they can manage to do is hate others.
It is no wonder that they are tearing the world to bits.

Half the Population

Half the Population is locked up.
And the other half really ought to be.
You have heard about the firefighters.
And you have heard about the doctors and nurses.
And believe me these are the good guys.
There are rogue taxi drivers everywhere.
People on your street are domestic abusers.
The world is in a terrible state because of this.
You may think I am the one who is badly behaved.
Well, hello to the rest of you out there.
At least you are mostly at work.
And you have to pay for the likes of me.
Who continues to try but cannot get on?
Because there never enough time to get well
And you never wanted me to do anything anyway.
Half the world is locked up.
And the other half really should be.

Fools Go Crazy

Fools go crazy.
Sometimes you have no choice.
You need to learn to hate.
You need to use your voice.
When the best thing in life
Is going to have a shit.
You need to shrug your shoulders.
And get on with it.
I never made things easy.
I'm difficult to climb.
I do not care about them.
And I cannot always spare a dime.
Fools go crazy.
Sometimes you have no choice.
You really need to go to sleep.
And you do not have a choice.

Take Me Seriously

You need to take me seriously.
I have a frightening disability.
I lost my sense of humour.
But I will laugh if you want to
All I do is ignore people.
I do not have anything to say.
I had some conversation.
But they took it all away.
I am still the same person.
I have already been to prison.
I do not want to go back.
I had better stay on the track.
And you had better get off my back.

Reset Myself

It's been another difficult Christmas.
And its not quite over yet
Our grandson still needs his present.
And I have still got things to get.
I have ended up being quite ill.
And I am not over it yet.
I need to lie awake and think tonight.
Most of all I need to press reset.
I need to go back to how I was.
Last week when I was well.
Do not bet all your money on an old nag.
Your horse won the race and fell.
I need to lie awake to have a rest.
If I am going to get back to what I do best

I Used to Bother

I used to bother to go to mental hospital.
When I was ill and needed a break from it
But all they did was keep me ill for years.
It was a waste of time and never made me well.
My illness and who I am is the problem here.
But they will not let me be anybody else.
They seem to have some sort of need for me.
Somebody to drive crazy and abuse at night.
Sometimes people really overstep the mark.
But I am better off having a bit of time to myself.
That is all I really need to be able to get better.
And at least they have the grace to leave me alone.
Nobody knows what to do about me anymore.
People give up and go away as time goes on.
I used to bother but little by little they are gone.

I See What I Want

I can see things my own way these days.
I have recently lost my glasses.
But I do not really need them that much.
I used to have a condition with my eyes.
When they were uncomfortable even when closed
I used to think I would be better off blind.
Because they hurt so much, and I was in pain.
That is what the mental health profession did for me.
I had twenty years with the same problem.
But now I can see reasonably well although not perfectly.
I can see what I like and what I do not.
I can see I have come far and what I have got.

Mentally Ill

For some people being mentally ill is their best bet
It is all they can do and get on with doing.
I am one of these people who do not fit.
I would go out and get a job if I could do it.
My disability means I am not suitable for anything.
I need balls of steel to go to the supermarket.
Never mind drive to work and do a job.
Some people in the government think I should be working.
But they are ignorant idealists who understand nothing.
The mental health profession made me an addict.
They give you CBT and say you are cured now.
What do they do when you cannot talk to them?
Because they do not want to listen and cannot help
I am mentally ill but do not belong in a hospital.
Give me money and pills and I can get on.

Andrew Aldred

Hope

Sometimes all we have is hope.
That the war in Israel will stop
That Ukraine and Russia will make peace.
That the weather might improve
And that we can carry on another day
There will be a world left for our children.
And we will not ruin it completely.
In self-interest and short-term profit
I hope people will leave me alone.
And let me get along with my girlfriend.
But it is up to me to make the effort.
Only you can make your situation better.
And I carry on trying every day.
I still bother to write you this poetry.
I deserve to be heard like everyone else.
I have some hope for the future.
I hope you have some dreams as well.
Do not let the world take them away.

www.ingramcontent.com/pod-product-compliance
Lightning Source LLC
Chambersburg PA
CBHW030049100426
42734CB00037B/703